09-BHK-642

Pebble® Bilingüe/ Bilingual Plus

Dientes sanos/Healthy Teeth

Un diente está flojo !
Loose Tooth

por/by Mari Schuh

Traducción/Translation:
Dr. Martín Luis Guzmán Ferrer

Editor Consultor/Consulting Editor:
Dra. Gail Saunders-Smith

Consultor/Consultant:
Lori Gagliardi CDA, RDA, RDH, EdD

CAPSTONE PRESS
a capstone imprint

Pebble Plus is published by Capstone Press,
151 Good Counsel Drive, P.O. Box 669, Mankato, Minnesota 56002.
www.capstonepress.com

092009
005618CGS10

Books published by Capstone Press are manufactured with paper
containing at least 10 percent post-consumer waste.

Library of Congress Cataloging-in-Publication Data
Schuh, Mari C., 1975-
    [Loose tooth. Spanish & English]
    Un diente esta flojo = Loose tooth / por Mari Schuh.
    p. cm. — (Pebble Plus bilingüe. Dientes sanos = Pebble Plus bilingual. Healthy teeth)
    Summary: "Simple text, photographs, and diagrams present information about having a loose tooth,
including how they feel and how to take care of all teeth properly — in both English and Spanish" — Provided
by publisher.
    Includes index.
    ISBN 978-1-4296-4598-0 (lib. bdg.)
    1. Teeth — Mobility — Juvenile literature. 2. Teeth — Care and hygiene — Juvenile literature. I. Title. II.
Title: Loose tooth.
RK63.M36818 2010
617.6'01 — dc22   2009040923

Editorial Credits
Sarah L. Schuette, editor; Katy Kudela, bilingual editor; Adalin Torres-Zayas, Spanish copy editor;
    Veronica Bianchini, designer; Eric Manske and Danielle Ceminsky, production specialists

Photo Credits
Capstone Press/Karon Dubke, all

The author dedicates this book to her parents, Mona and Daniel Schuh, of Fairmont, Minnesota.

Note to Parents and Teachers

The Dientes sanos/Healthy Teeth set supports national science standards related to
personal health. This book describes and illustrates what it's like to have a loose tooth in
both English and Spanish. The images support early readers in understanding the text.
The repetition of words and phrases helps early readers learn new words. This book also
introduces early readers to subject-specific vocabulary words, which are defined in the
Glossary section. Early readers may need assistance to read some words and to use the
Table of Contents, Glossary, Internet Sites, and Index sections of the book.

Table of Contents

Tabla de contenidos

Teeth

Having a loose tooth is part of growing up. Andy was 5 when his first baby tooth became loose.

Los dientes

Tener un diente flojo es parte del crecimiento. Cuando Andrés tenía 5 años se le aflojó su primer diente de leche.

A permanent tooth inside Andy's gums pushed on his baby tooth. The loose tooth fell out.

El diente permanente dentro de la encía de Andrés empujó hacia afuera el diente de leche. Entonces el diente flojo se le cayó.

A permanent tooth grew into the empty space. Andy will have 32 permanent teeth when he is an adult.

Un diente permanente creció en el espacio vacío. Andrés tendrá 32 dientes permanentes cuando sea adulto.

How It Feels

Having loose teeth can feel funny. Andy has two loose teeth that he wiggles with his tongue.

Cómo se siente

Se siente muy extraño tener un diente flojo. Andrés tiene dos dientes flojos que menea con la lengua.

Loose teeth make it hard to eat some foods. Andy has trouble biting into a hard apple.

Los dientes flojos dificultan comer algunos alimentos. Andrés tiene dificultad para morder una manzana dura.

Andy eats soft foods
like yogurt instead.

Andrés come alimentos
blandos como el yogurt.

Nutrition Facts

Serving Size
1container (142g)
Servings 1
Calories 100
Fat Cal. 0

*Percent Daily Values (DV) are
based on a 2,000 calorie diet.

Amount/Serving	%DV*	Amount/Serving	%DV*
Total Fat 0g	0%	Total Carb.22g	
Sat. Fat 0g	0%	Fiber 0g	
Trans Fat 0g		Sugars 0g	
Cholest. 0mg	0%	Protein 5g	
Sodium 70mg	3%		

Vitamin A 0% • Vitamin C 0% • Calcium 0% •

INGREDIENTS: CULTURED NONFAT MILK, SUGAR, STRAWBERRY FRUIT BASE (HIGH
FRUCTOSE CORN SYRUP, STRAWBERRIES, WATER, SUGAR, FOOD STARCH-MODIFIED,
CITRIC ACID, NATURAL FLAVOR, RED 40), FOOD STARCH-MODIFIED, GELATIN, POTASSIUM SORBATE (A PRESERVATIVE).

THIS ENTIRE PACKAGE IS COPYRIGHTED ©2004 KEMPS, LLC
GENERAL OFFICES, MINNEAPOLIS, MN 55414
www.kemps.com CONSUMER HOTLINE 1(800) 726-9455
ACTIVE YOGURT CULTURES GRADE A • PASTEURIZED. PURE CULTURE

Loose teeth sometimes hurt a little. Andy's mouth feels better in a few days.

Algunas veces los dientes flojos duelen un poco. La boca de Andrés se siente mejor en unos días.

Healthy Teeth

Having healthy teeth means having a healthy smile. Andy makes sure he brushes and flosses every day.

Dientes sanos

Tener dientes sanos significa tener una sonrisa sana. Andrés tiene cuidado de lavarse y usar el hilo dental todos los días.

You can take care of your teeth too. Soon, you'll have a whole new smile!

Tú también puedes cuidarte los dientes. ¡Muy pronto tendrás toda una nueva sonrisa!

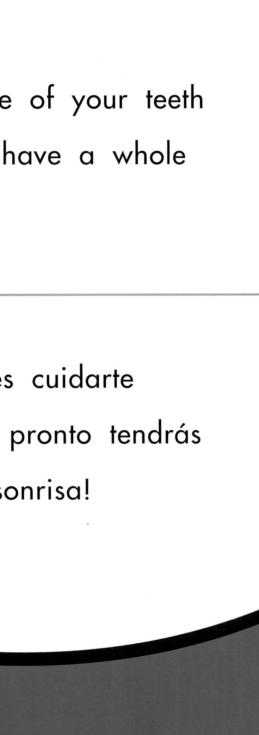

Glossary

baby teeth — the first teeth you have; baby teeth are also called primary teeth.

floss — to pull a thin piece of dental floss between your teeth to help keep your teeth clean

gum — the firm skin around the base of teeth

permanent teeth — the teeth you have your whole life, after your baby teeth; permanent teeth are also called adult teeth.

tongue — a muscle in your mouth you can move

wiggle — to move something up and down or side to side just a little bit

Internet Sites

FactHound offers a safe, fun way to find Internet sites related to this book. All of the sites on FactHound have been researched by our staff.

Here's all you do:

Visit *www.facthound.com*

FactHound will fetch the best sites for you!

Glosario

los dientes de leche — los primeros dientes que te salen; los dientes de leche también se llaman dientes primarios.

los dientes permanentes — los dientes para toda tu vida, que te salen después de los dientes de leche; los dientes permanentes también se llaman dientes de adulto.

la encía — piel firme que rodea la base del diente

la lengua — músculo en la boca que puedes mover

limpiarse los dientes con hilo dental — uso de un pedazo de hilo delgado que se introduce entre los dientes para mantenerlos limpios

menear — mover un poquito una cosa de arriba a abajo o de lado a lado

Sitios de Internet

FactHound brinda una forma segura y divertida de encontrar sitios de Internet relacionados con este libro. Todos los sitios en FactHound han sido investigados por nuestro personal.

Esto es todo lo que tú necesitas hacer:

Visita *www.facthound.com*

¡FactHound buscará los mejores sitios para ti!

Index

índice